75ᵖ

Roger Forster
SAVING FAITH

D1550239

Scripture Union
130 City Road, London EC1V 2NJ

© Roger Forster 1984

First published 1984

ISBN 0 86201 220 1

Bible quotes marked NIV are from the Holy Bible, New International Version. Copyright © 1973, 1978, International Bible Society.

Bible quotes marked GNB are from the Good News Bible – Old Testament: Copyright © American Bible Society 1976; New Testament: Copyright © American Bible Society 1966, 1971, 1976.

Bible quotes marked RSV are from the Revised Standard Version of the Bible, copyrighted 1946, 1952 and © 1971 by the Division of Christian Education, National Council of the Churches of Christ in the USA and used by permission.

Bible quotes marked NASB are from the New American Standard Bible, © The Lockman Foundation 1960, 1962, 1963.

Phototypeset by Wyvern Typesetting Limited, Bristol

Printed and bound in Great Britain at
The Pitman Press, Bath

Contents

Introduction

'Salvation' is the only word which is big enough, strong enough, tough enough and radical enough to challenge the current world situation and to be a message of any use to the human race today.

Of course there are those who still have plenty of 'good advice' about world affairs, lifestyles, even our relationships with the domestic and psychological problems they bring. Others direct our attention to supposed 'good economics' as though cash flow solves all. 'Good defence' is thought by some to be the answer to world conflicts; sophisticated destructive weapons that keep a balance of power are fondly thought to resolve both national and personal tensions. Most people's response to such simplistic solutions however is 'good heavens', 'good grief', or even 'good Lord!'

Perhaps this last exclamation is nearest the heart of the problem as well as being its solution. At least Christians claim so. It is because we have a good Lord that there is good news for all people. In fact, the goodness of this God is seen in the title he was given when he visited this planet nearly 2,000 years ago, to begin a rescue operation aimed at resolving our predicament. 'Don't be afraid! I am here with good news for you which will bring great joy to all the people. This very day, in David's town, your *Saviour* was born – Christ the Lord! (Luke 2:10, 11, GNB). The message, the manifestation and the movement begun by God was, in a word, salvation, or the Saviour. What God says, reveals, and does is all in a person, Jesus Christ. In fact, the name given to this person was 'Jesus' as the well-known Christmas story tells us in Matthew 1:21. It was declared, 'You will name him Jesus because he will save his people from their sins' (GNB). 'Jesus' means 'the Lord saves'

5

and is the Greek form of the Hebrew word *Yeshua*. In its Jewish form the word *Yeshua* appears in many places, as though the Old Testament prepared the Jews for their coming king by writing 'Jesus' all over their scriptures, especially when they spoke of God's great rescue operation. Isaiah gives an example of this –

God is my saviour;
  I will trust him and not be afraid.
The Lord gives me power and strength;
  he is my saviour.
As fresh water brings joy to the thirsty,
  so God's people rejoice when he saves them.

                                        Isaiah 12:2–4, GNB

But we could equally accurately read this as –

God is my Jesus;
I will trust him and not be afraid.
The Lord gives me power and strength;
He is my Jesus.
As fresh water brings joy to the thirsty,
So God's people draw water from the wells of Jesus.

Similarly, Psalm 9:14 may read, 'I will rejoice in your Jesus'. Try substituting 'Jesus' for 'deliverance', or 'save' in Genesis 49:18, Isaiah 62:11, Habbakuk 3:13. Jesus, when he came, embodied all the Old Testament prophecies concerning salvation.

Some people are unnecessarily embarrassed by the word 'salvation', even by the word 'saved'. To ask 'are you saved?' is thought to be outdated religious jargon with no real meaning. But survivors from an air crash are enthusiastic in telling us how they were saved. The word certainly means something to them. A meal saved for you if you are late home is a mark of love and care, not an embarrassment. So why should we think that 'saved', in a Christian context, is hard to understand? However, if we substituted a coined word like 'Jesus-ed' ('Are you Jesus-ed?'), the point would be very clear and equally true for a real Christian. The real Christian is a 'Jesus-ed' person. The prophecy did say that God would put his name on us and to carry the name 'Jesus' would be no different from carrying the name 'Christian' as we do when we say we are Christians. A Jesus-ed person is saved and a saved person is in Christ Jesus!

1
Full salvation

Looking at salvation more closely, the Bible describes those who trust in Christ as 'saved', 'being saved' and 'shall be saved'.

We are *saved* from the penalty, or consequences, of *sin* which is a distintegrating and deadening effect on our spirits making us unresponsive to God and his love. The consequences and judgement of sins are removed by Christ's work and we are made alive to God.

Look up: 2 Timothy 1:9; Ephesians 2:5; Titus 3:5.

We are *being saved* from the power of *sin* in our souls, as the character of Jesus is reproduced in our personalities and the magnetic field of sin is overcome by Jesus's Spirit in us enabling righteousness to be fulfilled in us.

Look up: 1 Corinthians 1:18.

We *shall be saved* from the presence of *Satan* and *sin* and the temptations to which our body's presence on earth exposes us. With our resurrection bodies we shall be finally, totally and comprehensively saved. Even now our bodies experience salvation when they are 'made alive' or 'healed', so anticipating the final future tense 'We shall be saved'.

This is dramatically demonstrated in the interwoven stories of the woman who had internal bleeding for twelve years and the twelve-year-old daughter of Jairus who was raised from the sleep of death. Both are found in Mark 5:21–42. The woman was commended, 'My daughter, your faith has saved you', referring to her healing. Then Jesus further demonstrated his power to 'save' and give life to the body by raising Jairus's daughter from death.

Look up: Romans 13:11; 8:11; Mark 5:34; Acts 4:10.

Just as the kingdom of God is spoken of as having *come* (Matthew 4:17), *coming* now (Romans 14:17) and yet *to come* in the future (Revelation 11:15; Matthew 6:10), so also the Bible teaches us that salvation has a past, present and future aspect. Paul tells us that we are those upon whom the 'ends of the ages have come' (1 Corinthians 10:11, RSV). By this expression he means that the *old age* – called an 'evil age' (Galatians 1:4), and the *new age* – God's age, 'the home of righteousness' (2 Peter 3:13, NIV), are overlapping at present in our experience. We are living in this overlap, experiencing still the effects of the old age, but being saved from it by participating in the powers of the coming age (Hebrews 6:5). We could illustrate this by a diagram like this:

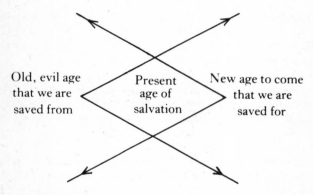

Old, evil age that we are saved from

Present age of salvation

New age to come that we are saved for

Paul promises us that we shall be saved in this life. The rescue operation of God is entered into and so enters into us when we put our trust in Christ. His life then begins to permeate all we are doing and ultimately all that we ever shall be.

As we start from this position of 'saved' and experience in our spirits, souls and bodies the saving life of Christ ('being saved') and rejoice in looking towards the future hope of 'shall be saved', we affect the world in which we live. This life which is in us spreads out into our relationships and our environment, changing things there even as it is rescuing and transforming our own lives. Church life, or Christian community living, is participating in corporate salvation. It also enriches our lives and, in turn, this affects the secular society wherever we touch it and move in it.

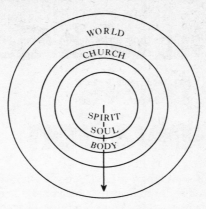

So ripples of salvation begin to invade the territory of the enemy's world like shock troops storming in on evil, unbelief, ignorance and every form of human depravity and oppression. This invasion of the world is not accomplished by our destructive violence or human cleverness, but by the presence and power of Jesus's life in us and through us, subduing the world by his influence, just as when he was on earth. 'Our life in this world is the same as Christ's' (1 John 4:17, GNB). How this salvation invasion spreads through the earth, how the church together expresses and exerts its influence, how an individual grows and develops as a source of salvation life, by faith, obedience and proclamation of the word of salvation must all be examined as our book proceeds.

2

Right with God: the basis of salvation

After years of searching for God, John Wesley heard Martin Luther's introduction to Romans being read. He felt his heart strangely warmed as he knew and felt that he believed. Salvation, like a fire, spread through him and his companions and throughout the British Isles in the eighteenth century, radically changing the lifestyle of the British people and, in some historians' opinion, 'saving us' from a revolution of the sort that occurred in France.

Luther himself had written his book out of his experience of being saved. At the time of his conversion he was lecturing on the Epistle to the Romans, which speaks of salvation and faith. The colossal social upheavals of the Reformation which were to alter the face of Europe were born out of this time as Luther began to grasp the meaning of God's righteousness as he saw it in Romans 1:16, 17:

I have complete confidence in the gospel; it is God's power to save all who believe, first the Jews and also the Gentiles. For the gospel reveals how God puts people right with himself: it is through faith from beginning to end. As the scripture says, 'The person who is put right with God through faith shall live.' (GNB)

How could Luther be put right with God when he was confronted by God's righteousness? If God was righteous and just, Luther knew himself condemned. He was unrighteous and no number of penances and good works, self denials or religious activities could take away the paralysis which the thought of God's justice brought to bear on him. How could there be any hope, any justification, for somebody like him? As light dawned in his soul he saw that the justice of God would not condemn him but would, if he had faith, release him into the freedom of a child of God (see Romans 8:21). God had made a way through the death of his son Jesus that would enable God himself to remain righteous and yet make Luther, and anyone who wanted to believe, right with him also. To be justified is to be made right with God, or righteous. (The two words are the same in Greek).

> God did this in order to demonstrate that he is righteous. In the past he was patient and overlooked people's sins; but in the present time he deals with their sins, in order to demonstrate his righteousness. In this way God shows that he himself is righteous and that he puts right everyone who believes in Jesus. (Romans 3:26, GNB)

Luther saw that it is the one who trusts the faithfulness of Jesus, not the one trusting in his own righteousness, who has the right to be taken up by God's salvation programme.

Many men and movements before and since Luther have rediscovered the explosive power of God's salvation received by faith, as revealed in these verses. Peter Waldo, John Wycliffe and John Huss begin a list which could continue for pages down to the present day.

Let us make sure that we too are involved in the great flow of God's salvage programme for mankind, which is destined to reach the ends of the earth before the final wave of salvation comes with the appearing of our Lord Jesus Christ, at the end of the age (Hebrews 9:28).

This is the good news. It means that in this message of salvation God's righteousness is revealed. Because of Jesus Christ's voluntary death on our behalf, God forgives us and puts us right with him.

We are like men retreating from a forest fire, who are saved by someone starting a second fire on unburnt ground. As the main fire sweeps towards them they are able to stand on the bare patch left by the second fire, and so the flames, finding nothing to consume, sweep round and past them and they are saved. So the Bible says we shall not come into judgement, but

11

are passed from death to life. God's fire of anger at sin has passed over us, scorching Christ and freeing us. Romans 5:9 says, 'By his death we are now put right with God; how much more, then, will we be saved by him from God's anger!' (GNB).

It is only as we are sure that the death of the Lord Jesus Christ has provided a safe ground for us to stand before God that we have the confidence to enter by faith through the power of the Holy Spirit into the saving life of Christ. We could illustrate it like this:

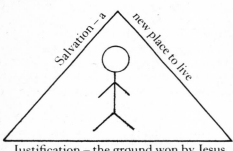

Justification – the ground won by Jesus

Another way in which the New Testament speaks of our position is in terms of cleansing. We stand before God with nothing offensive to God since Christ's blood has purified us from every sin (1 John 1:7). So Jesus says, 'Neither do I condemn you' as a prelude to 'go and sin no more' (John 8:1–11). Paul adds 'There is no condemnation now for those who live in union with Christ Jesus . . . so that the righteous demands of the Law might be fully satisfied in us who live according to the Spirit, and not according to human nature' (Romans 8:1,4, GNB). Too many sincere people live lives which appear not very different from their less sincere neighbours because, for all their church-going and commitment to Christian things, they have little or no confidence that God has accepted them, or that they are in good standing with God. In fact, some would think it proud or conceited of them to assume they were. The good news of salvation is to remove this uncertainty so that we feel secure in God. Assured of our acceptance by God through Christ's death for our sins, any man or woman may enter into a whole new sphere of existence where there is deliverance from fears and Satan, help in time of need, health for our whole person and beauty in the place of so much ugliness. This enrichment of life is because of Jesus Christ of whom it says: 'Rich as he was, he made himself poor for your sake, in order to make you rich by means of his poverty' (2 Corinthians 8:9, GNB).

Jim was in his thirties, and had been in Christian circles all his life. He had been through a Bible School and was sincere in his faith as far as he could understand. He also had a good intellectual grasp of the doctrine of salvation. However, his life never seemed 'on top'. Life lived him; he certainly never lived life. He knew Paul said that the Christian reigns in life by Christ Jesus (Romans 5:17), but this was hardly his condition. After much prayer and counselling, in a sensitive moment of confession and with terrible self-loathing, Jim shared what was deeply inside him and had never been expressed before. He lived and thought things in his fantasy life which Christ, in his purity, could never be at home with. His love and admiration for Jesus only heightened his certainty that Jesus could have nothing to do with him, no matter how much he might want it. Nothing could shift this sense of self-loathing and rejection by God until he was told, and he accepted, that when Jesus was on the cross he was made equally offensive.

Jesus was made sin for us. He knew and tasted all that sin is and does as he cried out on the cross – 'My God, my God, why have you forsaken me?' It was because Jesus knew this at first hand that he could forgive and justify us (Isaiah 53:11). He knew what he was forgiving. The reaction of the pure to the impure was tasted by Jesus himself, who, as the offended one, yet stood in the place of the offender so that the condemnation and rejection could be received into himself instead of passing to us. Jim could trust forgiveness from someone like that – someone who knew him better than he knew himself. As he welcomed and thanked Jesus for what he now realised Jesus had offered him all his life – forgiveness of his fantasy life – he began to experience for the first time the power of salvation. His life has changed to one of fulfilment. New gifts and abilities are emerging as shame is disappearing and a sense of self-worth has grown from his enjoyment of living life in God's power.

3
Salvation in the Old Testament

The Bible is our source book for understanding God's programme and work in this world. However, although the first Christians knew the story of Jesus in much the same form as we know it (i.e. the four Gospels) it was known by word of mouth. To understand more deeply what the story meant and was still meaning, they turned to what God had already told them, written down in their histories, songs, prophecies and laws. In other words, the Bible of the first Christians was the Old Testament.

In this chapter, we are putting ourselves in the same situation as they were in, asking what does salvation mean for us now that Christ has come? What should we expect in the light of the preparation given in the Old Testament?

The first use of this word, salvation, is when Jacob in Genesis 49 blesses his sons and speaks of what will come to pass, through them, in later days. Many of the predictions concern sin and its consequences, but suddenly after one such statement about his son, Dan's, character, Jacob bursts out in the middle of all those negative comments with: 'I have waited (hoped) for your salvation, O Lord'. He knows that the seed of the world's blessing and salvation was promised through his grandfather, Abraham, his father, Isaac, and now himself: 'In your seed shall all the nations of the earth be blessed'. So, with all his strength and the illumination and energy of God's spirit, he asserts his faith in the final outcome of that seed, the coming Messiah, who brings salvation to all the nations of the earth, and, in hope, he rises above all the inadequate futures he has to prophesy for the majority of his sons. Jacob states his confidence in the coming salvation, but also declares it has not yet come. He doesn't really experience it yet. He is like many today who, surrounded by violence, anger, division, hard labour, oppression and slavery, deceit, hatred and exploitation (see Genesis 49:3–27) know these will continue, yet hope for something better. For Jacob, as for Christians today, this hope is not just the longing in the human heart for something better in mankind, but it is a hope based on God's promise that salvation (Jesus) will come. So it is a sound hope and not a rainbow-end pursuit. In fact, in Galations 3:13,14, Paul gives us even more encouragement by claiming that we, unlike Jacob, can experience that salvation now! For 'by becoming a curse for us Christ has redeemed us from the curse that the Law brings; for the scripture says, "Anyone who is hanged on a tree is under God's curse!" Christ did this in order that the blessing which God promised to Abraham might be given to the Gentiles by means of Christ Jesus, so that through faith we might receive the Spirit promised by God' (GNB).

As we move out of Genesis (the seed plot of the Bible, where all God's thoughts are planted), we come to the second instance where salvation appears, this time in Exodus, at the passing of Israel through the Red Sea. It is not the salvation for which Jacob waited – the coming seed of Abraham to bless the nations – but rather an event in Israel's history which illustrates the first of three Old Testament meanings of the word.

Salvation is deliverance from an enemy (Exodus 14:13; 15:2)

As the children of Israel saw themselves hemmed in by hills, swamps, and Pharaoh's armies, there was only one way forward – through the sea. Moses was told to speak the word, stand still and he would see the salvation of God. When Israel had passed through the sea on dry ground and the Egyptian army had drowned, the Israelites sang that God had fought and reigned on their behalf and that he who was their strength and song had become their salvation (Exodus 14:14–25; 15:3,18). So it is not surprising that when Jesus came speaking of the reign or kingdom of God, he defined it as bringing deliverance

15

to the captives, spoiling the defeated strong man's (Satan's) goods and unloosing those bound by sin and Satan (Luke 4:18,19).

Paul reminds Timothy in 2 Timothy 2:25,26 that by repentance and acknowledging this truth of Jesus, men may escape from the snare of the devil, who captures men to do his will.

Sometimes the damaging grip of the devil on people's lives stems from bad parental influence or neglect. Obviously, people are subjected to, and therefore become victims of, this sort of influence from their earliest years.

General deliverance

Alan was a young man whose father had abandoned him and his mother in his early years. This experience resulted in great anger and aggression which would break out uncontrollably. Deviant sexual drives haunted him. He tried to make relationships, but found they brought only fear and isolation. He writes: 'Since we prayed together, there really has been a deep healing and a phenomenal transformation! The deep depression has gone, along with my fear in reaching out to people. A deep happiness is emerging and for the first time in my life I feel peaceful. I am 'soaking' my mind in order to 'renew my mind'. I have been under considerable satanic attack, yet, claiming God's armour, I've come through to fight another day. My relationships have been transformed, I am now able to reach out and love the way I want to. Praise God!'

There are many areas where people today need deliverance. What about addiction, to smoking, drugs, even gambling, deliverance from occult involvement or from various influences in the past? Look at chapter four for a closer examination of the whole area of deliverance, and a worksheet of gospel references to this subject.

More generally Paul describes mankind's need for deliverance in Romans 7:7-25. Here he does not refer to man's slave master, Satan, by name, but writes of sin as though it were a person: sin found its chance (11); sold as a slave to sin (14). If I do what I don't want to do, this means that I am no longer the one that does it; instead, it is sin that lives in me (17).

This universal slavery to sin is as real as Israel's slavery to Egypt and both situations required a rescue operation to deliver their victims into freedom. For Israel in Exodus it was called salvation. So also it is for the Christian, who is 'saved' from sin by Jesus.

Paul's description in this passage of Satan's sphere of influence is as though it were a magnetic field of sin. It is as though individual acts of sinning build up metal in our hearts which will always be caught by the magnetic sin force in Satan's direction. This makes us go wrong even when we want to go right. 'I don't do what I would like to do, but instead I do what I hate' (15, GNB). 'For even though the desire to do good is in me, I am not able to do it' (18). This power that sin has is called the law of sin (23,25) and makes Paul, and any man who has tried to do good and right things, cry out, 'Who will rescue me?' (24). He provides the answer to his own question, an answer born out of his experience: 'Thanks be to God who does this through our Lord Jesus Christ'.

Here is man's condition:

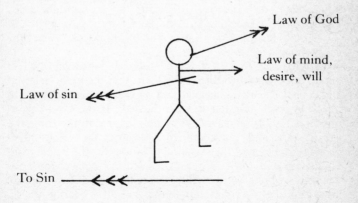

When, like Paul, we begin to worship and thank God for Jesus and what he has done and will do, a new force called the law of the Spirit comes into operation and now we experience freedom from sin's magnetic backward pull.

Here is the Spirit-led man advancing in obedience to God.

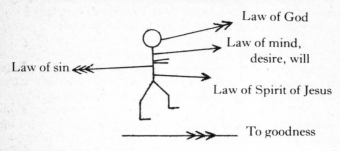

Salvation is help and health

In Psalms 42 and 43, the Psalmist is obviously low in spirits and encourages himself to trust in the Lord. 'Why am I so sad? Why am I so troubled? I will put my hope in God, and once again I will praise him, my saviour and my God' (GNB). The word translated 'saviour' here is expressed rather attractively in the King James Version as 'the health of my countenance'. Depression leaves its mark on our face, but the saving work of the Lord in our lives and hearts produces a healthy countenance.

Similarly, in Acts 14:9, when Paul healed the man who had been lame from birth, the text tells us that the man 'believed and could be healed', because that is exactly what happened to him. However, the actual word 'healed', is the Greek word normally translated 'saved'. The point is that in the Bible the words translated 'salvation' and 'healing' are often inter-changeable because the salvation of God is for the whole man, body, soul and spirit. We see this also in Isaiah chapter 53, when the prophet is foretelling the sufferings of Jesus on the cross in order to win salvation for us. As well as bearing our sin and punishment, he is described as bringing us healing by the blows he received (Isaiah 53:5).

These teachings of the Bible concerning salvation and healing have come to mean a lot to us as a family since my son was seriously ill with cancer two years ago. He was given less

18

than a one in five chance of survival, since the growths were disseminated throughout his body and in his central nervous system. After much prayer on his behalf we saw the situation turn around and all the growths disappeared. We then had to wait another week for the result of the test on his spinal fluid, to see what was happening there. During that time we kept praising the Lord for his intervention and expecting the spinal fluid to be free of malignant cells. On the morning we were due to get the results of the test, I read the two psalms already mentioned, Psalms 42 and 43. Immediately I knew that God was speaking to me. It was not what I wanted to hear, so at first I rejected it, but at last I gave in – God was telling me not to be discouraged and depressed by the news I would receive on arriving at the hospital: rather I was to hope in God who was the 'health of my countenance'. Sure enough, the news was bad. The test, we were told, showed that the central nervous system was much the same as at the beginning, before we had begun to pray. This turned out to be misinformation, but we did not know that for another two months. During that testing time my wife and I had the opportunity of positively putting our hope and trust in God and affirming that we would yet praise him, just as the Psalmist had exhorted us to do. As we did so, we found peace filling our hearts. Then later we heard that the information we had received was incorrect – the spinal fluid had in fact cleared up at the same time as the other growths were healed. But through this experience we proved afresh that God's salvation is spiritual, psychological and indeed physical wholeness and health.

Physical (Body)	Read Matthew 9:21,22,23; Mark 6:56; Matthew 14:36, Luke 8:50; 17:19; Acts 4:9; James 5:15. In all these verses the word translated healed or made whole is the word which means saved.
Psychological (Soul)	Read James 1:21; Romans 8:24; Jeremiah 14:8 (hope being a mark of health); Mark 8:35; (life = soul i.e. psyche).
Spiritual (Spirit)	Read Romans 5:9,10; 1 Corinthians 5:5; Ephesians 2:5,8 (our spirit is saved from the consequences of sin).

'May the God who gives us peace make you holy in every way

and keep your whole being – spirit, soul and body – free from every fault at the coming of our Lord Jesus Christ. He who calls you will do it, because he is faithful' (1 Thessalonians 5:23,24, GNB).

Salvation is beauty and glory

'He will beautify the afflicted ones with salvation' (NASB) says the Psalmist in Psalm 149:4. Isaiah also talks of 'beautifying' in 60:13, where he speaks of the glory of his house – that is, of course, his people, in whom he dwells. He explains that the bridal garments of salvation and the robe of righteousness are to be worn by his glorious people as a bride wears jewels and a bridegroom wears ornaments (Isaiah 61:10). God's salvation in Christ is not cold and austere, neither is it stark and clinical – it is a beautiful thing and makes those who get hold of it beautiful in their spirits and in their thoughts and actions. So Paul in Ephesians 5:22–27, having referred to Jesus as the Saviour of the church, proceeds to tell us that Christ is giving us a beautifying 'facial'. This is so that on the wedding day when he returns he will not have a bride with adolescent spots of immaturity or the old-age wrinkles of those bored or tired. The purity and faultlessness which salvation brings to the bride of Christ will be attractive to his gaze and to that of all the universe. Salvation means we are maturing and growing young at the same time. In order to 'appropriate' or take hold of this beauty we must first recognise and 'appreciate' it.

'Appreciation'

There is little doubt that Jesus Christ was extremely attractive when here on earth. My own first impression as a student – not yet a Christian – as I read Matthew, Mark and Luke was that Jesus was the sort of man I ought to be and, in my better moments, wanted to be. He was head and shoulders above any one I had ever met. I felt the beauty of his spirit as he said, 'I do not condemn you either. Go, but do not sin again' to the woman who was accused of adultery (John 8:11, GNB). I was moved by the look of friendship he gave to Peter, as Peter swore he never knew him, even though Jesus was about to be flogged and executed (Luke 22:61,62). I admired his courage in telling the story of the Good Samaritan (Luke 10:25–37), comparable only with telling the story of the 'Good PLO man' in Jerusalem or the 'Good IRA man' in the Shankhill Road today. I loved his action of putting a child in the circle of competing and self-assertive apostles with the words, 'Whoever welcomes this child in my name, welcomes me; and whoever welcomes me, also welcomes the one who sent me. For he who is least among you all is the greatest' (Luke 9:46–48, GNB). Even when the nails were driven through his hands and feet for execution, he said, 'Father forgive them; they don't know what they are doing'. That is beautiful. Let us take time to meditate, concentrate – to fill our minds with God's thoughts, with Jesus and his work. As we do this, we are setting the Lord before our face and thereby find he is at our right hand to strengthen and clothe us with himself to bring his beauty and goodness into our lives. (See Acts 2:25; Psalm 16:8–11.)

Appropriation

It is in this position and attitude of 'appreciation' that we are able to appropriate the same beauty or glory of salvation into our own lives.

Paul describes this process in 2 Corinthians 4:6 and 3:18: 'God, who said: "Out of darkness the light shall shine!" is the same God who made his light shine in our hearts, to bring us the knowledge of God's glory shining in the face of Christ.' As we look at him, 'All of us, then, reflect the glory of the Lord with uncovered faces; and that same glory coming from the Lord, who is the Spirit, transforms us into his likeness in an ever greater degree of glory' (GNB). The Christian's life is not just to be a 'right good one' but a beautifully good one. Maybe that is why when Jesus says in Luke 6:27,28 'Love your enemies, do good to those who hate you' he uses the word which means 'beautiful good' rather than plain 'good'. Further he says 'Bless', that is, 'Speak beautifully to' those who curse you. Such a great salvation is expressed in the words of the familiar song:

Let the beauty of Jesus be seen in me,
All His wondrous compassion and purity;
O Thou Spirit Divine,
All my nature refine,
Till the beauty of Jesus be seen in me.

Many times in the history of the church God has broken
into dry orthodoxy, dead formalism and crippling ecclesiastical
institutions, with his supernatural explosion of salvation. This
rescues us from mere conventional religion and warms our
hearts with life. 'We will be saved by Christ's life', Paul would
say (Romans 5:10). This infusion of life can be as dramatic and
as revolutionary as it must have seemed when the angels sang at
Bethlehem and announced, 'Unto you is born this day .. a
Saviour'. Or much quieter, but no less far reaching and
profound, as when Simeon took the infant Jesus in his arms and
said: 'Now let your servant depart in peace, for my eyes have
seen your salvation'.

Let us join in the prayer of St. Francis:

O Lord, our Christ, may we have your mind and your spirit;
Make us instruments of your peace;
Where there is hatred, let us sow love;
Where there is injury, pardon;
Where there is discord, union;
Where there is doubt, faith;
Where there is despair, hope;
Where there is darkness, light;
Where there is sadness, joy.

O divine Master, grant that we may not so much seek to be
        consoled as to console;
to be understood, as to understand;
to be loved, as to love;
for it is in giving that we receive;
it is in pardoning that we are pardoned;
and it is in dying that we are born to eternal life.

Amen.

4

Salvation
is deliverance

At the beginning of his ministry, Jesus announced his rescue plan:

> The Spirit of the Lord is upon me,
>> because he has chosen me to bring good news to the poor.
>
> He has sent me to proclaim liberty to the captives
>> and recovery of sight to the blind;
>
> to set free the oppressed
>> and announce that the time has come
>> when the Lord will save his people.

(Luke 4:18,19, GNB)

His manifesto concerned deliverance from poverty, captivity and oppression. This good news is not merely about freedom from the outward forms of these bondages in society, though these would be eroded by his power. Rather, starting from within, a person was to be delivered so that he might become in turn a deliverer; saved that he might bring salvation to others. We become 'saviours' – those who save – as we bring the life and power of Jesus to bear on the world. This is why it is prophesied in Obadiah 21 that saviours would come up on Mount Zion to bring justice to the people, and 'the kingdom shall be the Lord's'. It is as we bring salvation that we *reign* in life and *train* for the life to come. Christian living is *training* in salvaging in order to be *reigning* in the saved universe, when it will be said 'Now have come the salvation and the power and the kingdom of our God and the authority of his Christ' (Rev. 12:10, NIV).

The verse quoted at the end of the preceding paragraph is

23

from the book of Revelation which is the war book of the kingdom of God. The victory which is celebrated has come about because there has been a group of people – Christians – who have during their earthly life committed themselves totally to overcoming God's enemy, Satan. 'For the one who stood before our God and accused our brothers day and night has been thrown out of heaven' (Revelation 12:10, GNB). As we, with wills obedient to our Lord, use the twin forces of Christ's blood and his truth (or name, as it is said elsewhere, e.g. John 16:23,24) we defeat the accuser and release men and women from his grip. The power of these two weapons lies in what Jesus has done for us and requires our faith to be bold enough to risk everything in speaking them forth. As we declare the blood of Christ, the accuser has no grip of guilt on his victim for Christ's death has removed everything God had against him and the blood of Jesus purifies from all sin (1 John 1:7). So Satan loses the chain of guilt by which he holds people in defeat while they think God would not and could not have anything to do with them. Now such victims know that God is for them and loves them. When we boldly and authoritatively declare God's truth in Jesus into a situation, not only are we telling Satan's victims the promises of God but we are also reminding Satan of his defeat in the wilderness and at Calvary by our Lord Jesus. We remind him of this humiliation and also of Christ's exaltation.

And so, in honour of the name of Jesus all beings in heaven, on earth, and in the world below will fall on their knees, and all will openly proclaim that Jesus Christ is Lord, to the glory of God the Father.

Philippians 2:10–11 (GNB)

In the name of this same Jesus Satan must relinquish his demonic hold on his victims.

A desperate phone call brought a problem to my door one day. Jack was married, with children, but suffered from acute attacks of homosexual feelings. He felt ashamed as he hid his dilemma, guilty for his wife's sake and humiliated by his fight and continuing failure. Could Christ meet him in his need? That morning as we shared in the presence of God's love and acceptance in Christ, Jack wrote down a list of areas where he felt God's will was not being done in his life. My final question as I counselled him with a colleague was, 'Have you ever had any involvement with the occult?' 'None at all,' was his confident reply. 'Are you sure?' 'Well, I was levitated once, but it didn't mean anything to me' he answered. 'Let's put that down on the list too,' I said. We prayed together through the areas he had listed, calmly and coolly. However, as he began to pray about levitation, he became quite emotional. He was surprised at himself. As he tried quietly to ask God to forgive him and cleanse him from the levitational involvement, he suddenly burst into tears, much to his own astonishment. God had given my colleague some scriptures that morning as he had been in prayer. They were from the Psalms:

When I am surrounded by troubles,
    you keep me safe.
You oppose my angry enemies
    and save me by your power.

(Psalm 138:7, GNB)

He supplies the needs of those who honour him;
    he hears their cries and saves them.

(Psalm 145:19, GNB)

So together we asked the Lord Jesus to save Jack from the evil force that was oppressing his life. As we did so, Jack wept and continued to do so for twenty or thirty minutes. Since that day, he has never been afflicted by homosexual temptation again. If you asked him if he were saved, he would respond joyfully and positively, 'Yes!', and you would know that he had good reason to describe his condition in that way.

One of my most dramatic encounters with occult powers was when a member of a coven of witches came to my home. The man had been in a meeting in which I had been preaching and had behaved very strangely afterwards. As soon as I opened the front door to him he pointed at me and said, 'You are my enemy'. I'm afraid the only response this challenge evoked from me was, 'Oh, come in and have a cup of tea' – I'm not too original when it comes to quick repartee! After ten minutes of incoherent conversation, I managed to say 'Look, if you have come here to be delivered from that Satanist group, I can't do anything for you' – then I added, 'But Jesus Christ can'. At the mention of Jesus's name, the man either threw himself or was thrown by some alien force, across the room towards me. It is strange how, in the dramatic and traumatic moments of life, the most trivial and inconsequential things stand out in one's consciousness. In the middle of the room was our new coffee table with a glass top. My wife and I had saved up for a long time for this prized possession. As the man homed in on me, projected across the room, my first instinctive thought was, 'He's going to destroy our new coffee table!' Strangely – and to this day I don't know how – he missed it. My second unspiritual thought was, 'Praise the Lord, he's missed it!' My third consideration, taking thought for myself, was, 'Stand up, don't just sit there while he attacks you!' But as he hurtled to where I stood, he fell to the floor, beating it with his hands and feet. I pronounced deliverance over him in the name of Jesus, and eventually he became quiet and calm. I read the words of Psalm 51 to him, and he repeated them after me, particularly verses 1 and 4 (GNB).

Be merciful to me, O God,
     because of your constant love.
Because of your great mercy
     wipe away my sins!
I have sinned against you – only against you –
     and done what you consider evil.
So you are right in judging me;
     you are justified in condemning me.

And then verses 10–12:

Create a pure heart in me, O God,
     and put a new and loyal spirit in me.
Do not banish me from your presence;
     do not take your holy spirit away from me.
Give me again the joy that comes from your salvation,
     and make me willing to obey you.

One of the most outstanding things in this saving deliverance was that the twisted up face of this man was so completely changed that, as he left, my wife at first did not recognise him, although she had seen him when he had arrived. I might add that she had sat outside on the stairs praying and singing praise to Jesus while the encounter was going on in my study. My wife knew how important it is to surround ourselves and our children with the name of Jesus, which means salvation, in order to protect ourselves from demonic forces. 'The name of the Lord is a strong tower. The righteous run to it and are safe' (Prov. 18:10, NIV).

In Mark's gospel there is a particular focus on Christ's salvation programme with respect to deliverance. In all, there are fourteen instances which concern the confrontation with supernatural forces of evil which capture men in uncleanness and disabilities. Christ's commission to his apostles included authority over the dark side of the supernatural (Mark 6:7,13), and those who were also to believe are to have the same confidence in his name (Mark 16:17). These are those who, today, obey the same commission and seek to bring salvation to the world,

so that the whole world may know your will;
so that all nations may know your salvation.

(Psalm 67:2, GNB)

Worksheet

Look through Mark's Gospel, at the fourteen examples of deliverance given below.

1. 1:23–27	6. 3:22–30	11. 9:14–29
2. 1:32–34	7. 5:1–20	12. 9:38
3. 1:39	8. 6:7,13	13. 16:9
4. 3:10–12	9. 7:25–30	14. 16:17
5. 3:15	10. 8:33	

Are there areas in your own life where you still need the full deliverance that salvation brings? Think through areas of: addiction, occult involvement in the past, fantasy life, sexual sin, uncontrollable anger, fear, a spirit of rejection or resentment, lying or divination, an obsession with death or unhappiness, slavery to gambling, foul language and cursing. Anything in your life you are unable to control is slavery Jesus can, and wants to, break. Bring these things to the Lord in prayer and claim the promises from scripture mentioned in this chapter.

Make sure that, if you need further help and prayer, you do seek counselling with your own minister or a Christian whose life and faith you respect.

5
Salvation is help and health

We have already seen that in both the Old Testament and the New Testament, salvation is partly understood as health. In fact the AV says in Psalm 67:2: 'that your way be known upon the earth, your saving health among all nations'.

Also there are places in the Old Testament where the word 'salvation' has been translated simply 'help' as in 2 Samuel 10:11 (NASB), where Joab speaks of coming to help in battle: 'If the Syrians are too strong for me, then you shall help me, but if the sons of Ammon are too strong for you, then I will come to help you.'

In Psalm 3:2 where the Psalmist records that many enemies are troubling him with words meant to paralyse his soul – 'There is no help for him in God' – these negative words are words which we too have heard people say or felt the enemy say in our hearts.

Help and health are closely related in our lives. When we are sick, we readily admit we need help in a variety of ways. Moreover, good health is the greatest help we could hope for or imagine.

These two gifts, help and health, run intertwined through the verses of Psalm 41.

Verse 1 tells us God will help us when we are immersed in trouble.

Verse 2 explains how he helps. He will protect, preserve, make us happy and will not abandon us to our enemies.

Verse 3 continues to define the sort of help God is offering and states that he will help when we are sick and will restore our health.

Verses 4–9 further describe the trouble in which the Psalmist David is looking to God for help. He is feeling guilty because of his sins, he hears cruel things said about him, he feels the hatred of his enemies. No doubt these pressures have produced or at least contributed to the sickness to which he is subjected. He knows they are spreading bad news about him and hoping that his illness is fatal saying, 'He will never leave his bed'. Worst of all, even a best friend was acting treacherously. This was someone who had shared David's table; 'one who ate my bread has lifted up his heel against me' as some translations put it. This psalm is possibly born out of David's experience during the insurrection of his son, Absalom. Ahithophel, his trusted counsellor, defected to Absalom's side. When his counsel was rejected by Absalom and he knew that David would win and consequently his days were numbered, Ahithophel went out and hung himself (2 Samuel 17:23).

In John 13:18 Jesus quotes this verse and appropriately applies it to the traitor Judas who shared his table (see John 13:26), had his feet washed by Christ (John 13:5) and metaphorically had kicked his Master in the face when he betrayed him. Subsequently he hung himself, as did Ahithophel 1,000 years before. In these circumstances of his last hours on earth Jesus says that he was in trouble in his spirit because he was going to be betrayed by a close friend (John 13:21). Although we are unaware of Jesus ever suffering from illness until he was on the cross, the physical pressure at the time must have been stupendous. We know that in a short space of time after the Last Supper he was in Gethsemane in heaviness, sorrow, threat of death, even falling on the ground (Matthew 26:37–39). His agony and sweat seem extraordinary in their intensity (Luke 22:44). He needed heavenly help to strengthen and physically uphold him (Luke 22:43). This provision of help in trouble, and the physical ensuring of health and strength to go on to the crucifixion was given by the Father to Jesus. As God's power was available to Jesus, and to David, so it is for us today.

Health and help are at hand for those who are being saved in Christ's life (Romans 5:10). 'For if while we were enemies, we were reconciled to God through the death of His Son, much

29

more, having been reconciled, we shall be saved by His life' (NASB).

Already, as we have seen, the disintegrating power of God's displeasure has been removed from the believer. Notice in Romans 5:9 the 'much more'. 'By his death we are now put right with God; how *much more*, then, will we be saved by him from God's anger!' (GNB, see John 3:16,36; Romans 8:1). Consequently, we are to expect that God, being for us, will help us in our weakness and heal us from our disease.

I remember a man visiting a hospital and asking where his Christian friend was to be found. He received the reply from a staff member: 'He's in the third bed on the left, but you'll soon find him; he literally glows!' I suppose recovering in hospital from an accident was not too healthy in some ways, but spiritual life affects the body and even makes the face shine. Paul exhorts us (Romans 12:11) to be fervent, or spiritually aglow.

Healing of hurts

When we lose that glow and feel sick and heavy in our new life in Jesus, sometimes it is because God is seeking to deal with us in some deeper way, or aiming at some problem that has arisen which lessens our experience of his presence and goodness. All of us are the sum total of what we have inherited, experienced, said, felt – and done. It is into this web of experiences that God continues to break in with his saving health or inner healing. If your conversion to Christ was very dramatic, many of your main problems may have immediately been dealt with, but still there will be need, as you progress in the Lord, to find his touch in newer and deeper areas of your being. Alternatively, your conversion may have seemed very low-key in comparison to others whose stories you have heard, and it will be more immediately apparent to you that there is a long way yet to go in recovering the full health that 'Doctor Jesus' has come to give us.

Through our years of Christian ministry, my wife and I have counselled countless men and women who carry scars inside from past hurts and experiences. Some have had tragedies in their lives – the sudden death of a loved one, for example, perhaps a child, through illness or accident. We were once counselling a young man concerning guidance over a particular decision in his life. During the short time we had known him, we had often thought that he had an air of desolation about him at times and wondered about it. As we chatted over with him the factors concerning his future, silently praying that God would guide us, he quite abruptly burst into tears. On our gentle questioning as to what was troubling him, he replied that he did not know, but something was hurting him emotionally inside, and in the loving prayerful atmosphere of that moment it had burst out in that way. As he wept, we prayed again and then we began asking him about his childhood. It soon emerged that when he was only three years old he had seen his five-year-old brother killed in front of him when the boy had run under a tractor. He could only dimly recall the anguished cries and distress of his parents, but he could remember the awful desolation that had settled into his heart over the ensuing years. As a child he often lay awake thinking about his brother and what had happened to him. In teenage years and adulthood the memory had faded completely, but the hurt was still there, under the surface, affecting his adult life and emotions. As we prayed together with him he experienced the love of Jesus reaching out to the area of hurt and healing it.

Others have grown up in environments where they have experienced violence and sexual abuse. The reality of the saving power of Jesus has been our constant experience as we have prayed with such people and seen his love make damaged lives whole.

Healing of memories

When Jesus gave us the simple act of the communion or the Lord's Supper, he used the words, 'Do this in memory of me'. Our memories are important. They are a part of us. In fact we are made up of what we have received from our parents and environment, and what we have been, done, experienced, expressed and dreamed. We say this is our 'make up'. Out of this material, this memory bank (conscious or unconscious) of our being, we live. When we take the bread and wine of the communion, we are symbolically taking just what he is. His body is for us. Jesus says, 'Do this in memory of me', so that he can give us all of himself to invade our lives and memories.

When Paul declares triumphantly: 'I have been put to death with Christ on his cross, so that it is no longer I who live, but it is Christ who lives in me. This life that I live now, I live by faith in the Son of God, who loved me and gave his life for me' (Gal. 2:19–20, GNB), he is saying that his life has been involved with Christ's death and now he lives on Jesus's resources, that is his bank of memory, through his resurrection. Paul's history is now Jesus's history. Jesus added his cross to Paul's past and Paul now lives in Jesus's life added into his present.

Some of our memories, without Christ in them, are damaged and will damage us. In the Hebrew text of Proverbs 18:14 we read, 'The spirit of a man will sustain his infirmity but a wounded spirit who can bear?' If the very basis of our identity is damaged, our whole existence becomes insupportable. Life is a burden to bear, rather than an opportunity to be enjoyed and to enrich others as well as ourselves. Jesus's offer of bread and wine ministers into our inner man his life and death, history and memories and reminds us also of his death that sucked up sin into himself and made an end of it. Take the bread and wine and remember not your sin and your painful memories but me, he says. We take Christ into our memories and he heals and saves us from their damaging effects.

Pete had often been prayed for. He had personality problems, fears and a low self-image, which made him compete excessively. One night as two of us were praying with him, I described a room to him which I saw in my mind. He began to weep. He knew straight away it was the cloakroom outside the classroom of the school to which he had been sent as a boy. He hated the boarding school, resented his parents sending him there and told of being abused in that cloakroom by an older pupil. As we asked Jesus to enter into that memory and walk around it, relieving him of its bitterness and fear, God began a healing work, saving him from the tyranny of his past.

When we remember Jesus, as he commands us, we remember his cross. Here he was made sin for us, bore our sins or took up the sin of the world (2 Corinthians 5:21; 1 Peter 2:24; John 1:29). In this act Christ entered into all our own experiences of sinning. These experiences which have formed our memories are now also his with the addition that in him their judgement and execution have taken place. So he takes our memories and puts himself and his salvation into them while we take his life's experience of holy, truthful living and obedience to God and make that our own to live on day by day. 'It is no longer I who live, but Christ who lives in me.'

Many marriages are unsavable because of the hurtful and terrible things which have been said and done to each partner. These memories make reconciliation impossible unless they can be severed from the individuals. Sometimes it is asserted that such a cutting free from our past is outside the bounds of possibility. But in Christ this is feasible. So Paul says 'Get rid of your old self that made you live as you used to . . . and put on the new self'; the new self is Christ who is God's likeness and image, (Ephesians 4:22–24). Again in Colossians 2:11–15 the picture of circumcision – cutting away a bit of flesh – is used by Paul to show how the cross where Christ died is like a knife cutting away the old life. When our past lives and memories are given to God by faith, it means that just as our painful, evil memories are drawn into the crucifixion experience of Jesus, so their bad effects and condemnation are cut off through Calvary and we are freed from them so that we may live in Christ's life.

This was the experience of a young married couple who came to my wife and me on the first day of an annual Christian convention and bubbling over in excitement told us that it had been the best year of their lives. The year before, when we shared together, it had seemed impossible to erase the bad memories which were already tyrannising their marriage.

Another couple, John and Jean, were in their sixties and had divorced eight years before as incompatible. Jean came to Jesus; her ex-husband, now living on the other side of London, visited one Sunday and came with her to a worship service and, better still, to Christ. Their marriage, which they thought unredeemable, was salvaged and they are now happily remarried and using their home for a Christian house group.

Many women, and even some men, have only found relief from the guilt of an abortion when they have asked Jesus to enter into the experience, which haunts them from their past, bringing his forgiveness and his assurance of their child's forgiveness of the action, too. My wife and I were intrigued, when ministering to a woman haunted by an 'evil eye' in her imagination, to find that the early church spoke of aborted children fixing their eyes with reproach on their mothers, when they entered the after-life. We found that the lady concerned had had an abortion, but also that she seemed quite at peace and unconcerned about the matter. However, when we sought the Lord's forgiveness in prayer for the abortion, she wept and was 'saved' from her haunting eye.

Healing for the body

There is a whole army of Christian men and women throughout the world who will tell you how the Saviour made their bodies and minds whole. Joan, after years of hospitalisations for manic depression, was converted to Christ, who forgave her sin and began a new life in her. However, for a couple of years, though vastly helped, she still had minor doses of what she called 'the panics'. Some Christians suggested she abandoned her drugs completely, but my wife and I encouraged her to do so only when she was sure God had said so. One day after praying specifically concerning this matter, she 'chanced' to meet a stranger on the street, and fell into conversation with her. The lady turned out to be a Christian too. 'My dear', she told Joan, 'I've got so much to thank God for. You see, I was a manic depressive.' She then named the hospital and the ward where she had been treated, which was the very same hospital and ward that Joan had been in. Then she added, 'But the Lord has done so much for me. He has healed me and I don't take a single drug today.' Joan quickly thanked God in her heart, for she knew he was speaking to her through this stranger. She has never taken a drug for that condition since.

Bill, a married man with a family, was a real believer in Christ. He began to suffer bad headaches and the persistent pain eventually drove him to hospital. The X-rays revealed a brain tumour. That night we followed the instructions of James 5:14,15 where the Greek word 'save' is translated here as 'heal'. 'Is there anyone who is ill? He should send for the church elders, who will pray for him and rub olive-oil on him in the name of the Lord. This prayer made in faith will heal the sick person: the Lord will restore him to health, and the sins he has committed will be forgiven' (GNB).

Bill confessed all he knew of or understood as sin in his life. Love poured through the gathered group as we put oil on him, as a symbol of the Holy Spirit of Jesus. I felt that God put into my mind to say what would happen when he went into the hospital a few days later; that no growth would be found. However, I rather cautiously preceded my statement with the qualifying words, 'Wouldn't it be good if . . .'. Bill's pain left in two days. After X-rays in the hospital the following week he was sent home and received a letter with virtually the same words I had used – but without the cautious qualification! No tumour could be found. If you asked Bill today, 'Does Jesus save?', he would assure you in no uncertain terms!

Worksheet

The satisfaction of bringing salvation into others' lives is the most wonderful and fulfilling of experiences and you might enjoy it more than your own salvation!

So study the saving ministry of Jesus in the first half of John's Gospel. Look for these characteristics of a good doctor of souls. Ask God to make you an instrument in his operating hand.

1.	John 1:35–51	Attractive, confidence-building life.
2.	John 2:1–4	Enjoying others' interests.
3.	John 3:1–16	Willing to be inconvenienced.
4.	John 4:1–26	Unshockable.
5.	John 5:1–16	Willing to be misunderstood in order to save.
6.	John 6:15–21	Removing fear.
7.	John 7:1–17	Acting independently of pressures.
8.	John 8:1–11	Non-condemnatory.
9.	John 9:1–7	Hard and urgent worker.
10.	John 10:1–18	Self sacrificing.
11.	John 11:1–35	Compassionate and sympathetic.
12.	John 12:12–19	Can he use you?

6
Salvation is beauty

When Malcolm Muggeridge wrote about Mother Teresa and her work in Calcutta amongst the destitute, he called the book *Something Beautiful For God*. If you spoke to Mother Teresa about her service to disadvantaged mankind in India, she would almost certainly say it was something beautiful *from* God. Salvation beautifies life. Satan seeks to make it ugly. Salvation puts glory, honour and dignity on human beings. Satan's design is to have man damned in ugliness and shame, but God never intended human life to be without beauty. Reading Genesis 1 and 2 makes this very clear. Everything God made was good or very good and man's experience began in a garden, located in Eden – which means 'Delight'. It is sin and Satan's power that destroys and 'uglifies' life.

When we first experience salvation or deliverance, it might seem a little stark and austere. After all, we are cleaning up sin and the remedy is a traumatic one – the blood of Jesus. But even this is attractive and beautiful, because of the beauty of the person dying and the way he does it. All of us, when we are in heaven, will think like the hymn-writer who wrote: 'Those wounds, yet visible above, in beauty glorified'.

As we find Christ's saving life permeating our being, we might think the activity somewhat clinical, even if it is health-giving. But even here we get glimpses of Christ's character and wisdom in his guiding our lives, and bringing us to see our need and the provision he has made for us.

Salvation doesn't end there though, even if some people's 'religion' is both austere and clinical. God wants to get us into beauty and a life that makes beautiful.

My wife has caught something of this beauty which a saved and truly holy life should express in a meditation on the beautiful garments that Aaron, the Old Testament high priest, wore as recorded in Exodus 28:

What a glacial world we have made of His holiness,
remote and inaccessible as that far pole
whose unrelenting whiteness chills the soul
and numbs the senses . . .
where man who clings and strives with iron will
finds at the last he is an alien still,
and in some lonely spot the strongest fall
and leave no mark – snow swiftly covers all . . .
So why did God (who should have understood
how man would view such things)
choose for His model of the ultimate Good
– Aaron . . . . . . ?

He comes, he stuns the senses
blows the mind,
he wears
unutterable beauty as a breastplate
stones of fire
assail the eyes
their flashes starting pistols for the pulses . . .
ears are pierced exquisitely –
bells, bells,
ringing rapier-like but sweet . . .
And oh the fruit! mouth-watering luscious
pomegranates dripping juice
and tantalising visions of another Eden
(not lost this time but won) . . .

And tell me now, what human artistry
(for artists have a care for reputation)
would run amok with colours, blatant, bold,
then wrap the whole sense-stealing show in brightest gold
without restraint?
And who would dare
(breathe gently if you can)

to place such flagrant beauty on a mortal man,
then fasten to his forehead with a golden cord
    that stunning message –
        'HOLY TO THE LORD' . . . . . . ?

faith forster

There are two words in the Greek of the New Testament for 'good'. One means beautifully good. In the Epistle to Titus Paul uses this word four times and exhorts Titus to be an example of beautifully good behaviour (Titus 2:7). He also reminds him that the salvation which our great God and Saviour Jesus Christ has brought to mankind is in order that he should 'rescue us from all wickedness and make us a pure people who belong to him alone and are eager to do beautifully good things' (2:11–14). Again in 3:8,14 it is beautiful goodness which we must learn to do and give our time to.

The other word for 'good' indicates something that properly fulfils its designed purpose. Paul uses it in Ephesians 2:10 when he tells us that we have been saved and that 'God has made us what we are and in our union with Christ Jesus he has created us for a life of good deeds which he has already prepared for us to do' (GNB). But here he adds another slant. The Greek word used in this verse for 'made' sounds like 'poem', perhaps because, for the Greeks, anything that was made should be a work of art. So we are God's poem. It is quite remarkable how often, when people are converted, they become to their own surprise and everybody else's, a bit poetic. They begin to notice the beauty of creation when, before, they might have passed by without paying any attention. A Christian has awakened to a new world in which glory, honour and things that have everlasting value are the desired objectives (Romans 2:7). One hymn-writer described his experience in coming to Christ for salvation in these words:

> *Heaven above is deeper blue,*
> *Earth around is sweeter green,*
> *Something lives in every hue*
> *Christless eyes have never seen.*

I will never forget sharing a conference with an older man, a German, who had been imprisoned by the Nazis for his faith in

Christ. We stayed together in a Christian home. As we stood waiting for breakfast to be served, he said to me, 'Roger, those flowers,' pointing at an arrangement in the middle of the table, 'have been put there by loving hands.' Two and a half years of solitary confinement, brutality and torture had not coarsened his soul; rather Christ in him had opened his eyes to see God's beauty and to perceive it quickly in everything around him. That's all a part of being saved. There was also beauty in an experience he had had when he was told he had twenty-four hours to get out of Germany. The war with Britain was to be declared in a few days. Within hours of being in solitary confinement, he arrived at the airport penniless, but thinking it was the quickest way out of Germany. A man approached him, 'Are you Pastor S.?' – 'Yes'. 'The Lord told me to give you this, this morning', and he pushed an airticket to London into his hand, plus five pounds in English money. On arrival at London Airport, all Germans not having five pounds in English currency were being sent back to their own country. But imprisonment was not ended for him. When war broke out, he was imprisoned in the UK and again in Canada.

On returning to the UK after the war, Pastor S. began a preaching ministry throughout the country, expecting God to supply his needs as he promises in Philippians 4:19. One week-end he was due to start a series of meetings in a distant town and being again penniless, he asked God to send the wherewithal for a train ticket by the end of the week. Nothing came by that Friday. On Friday night he resolved, after a little struggle, to use, if he could, a gold half-sovereign that someone had given him as a memento. Next morning the post arrived – perhaps God had sent some cash for his ticket! But all that appeared was a parcel from a friend containing two bars of chocolate. Tossing one bar to the friend he lived with, he pocketed the other and went to the bank with his gold coin. They directed him to an antique shop, where he was paid the current price for his half-sovereign. Arriving at the station, he bought a ticket with all the money he had. This would take him part of the way to his destination. However, on the train, a craving for chocolate came over him. Pulling out the bar from his pocket, he proceeded to unwrap it, only to find a bank note slipped under the wrapper – a further gift from his friend.

When the guard came round, he was able to pay for another ticket to complete the journey. On arriving home, some fourteen days later, he asked the friend he lived with, 'Have you eaten your chocolate yet?' On receiving a negative reply, he found the second bar on the sideboard and opened it, but found no bank note! Salvation is beautiful because God is beautiful, and he clothes with his beauty our actions, relationships, speech and thoughts.

On hearing that a neighbour who had been conscripted into the Army was being court-martialled, a Christian travelled hundreds of miles at his own expense and gained an interview with the General with great difficulty and after much perseverance. He pleaded eloquently for his neighbour, spelling out his virtues, and offering whatever he could to meet the man's needs. The General was very impressed and offered to take all this into account when the court martial took place, concluding the interview with, 'You must love your friend very much, to go to such lengths on his behalf.' 'Oh, he is not my friend,' replied the Christian, 'he is my greatest enemy.' In the cause of justice alone, there is no necessity for loving so extravagantly, but salvation goes way beyond being just and fair only. Justice and fairness can be starkly cold and often self-righteous, storing up resentments and discontent. Salvation heaps beauty into ugliness, blessing where there is cursing, goodness into hatred, prayer in the face of persecution (Matthew 5:43–48).

Salvation's beauty is salvaging the world and countless lives from insipid mediocrity and boring drabness. Two sons of a Korean pastor died in a political riot. When the culprits were brought to trial, the pastor offered to take the under-age youths into his home in the place of his sons. One agreed to this and today is filling the earth with the news of Jesus. He has become – not surprisingly – an evangelist. Helmut, an East European communist leader was met and helped in the West by a young man who was the son of a pastor he had imprisoned. Eventually he became a Christian, dazzled by such forgiveness and love.

A century ago two thousand orphans were given a home by a man and his team whose appeal for supplies was only to God in prayer. On one occasion at the very moment when thanks were being given to God for the food they did not yet have, a baker brought bread to the orphanage. Having won some money on a boxing match the night before, he had arrived home to find his wife praying. 'I ought to do something for God,' he said, having one of those husbandly moments when he felt he wasn't worthy of such a good woman. 'Then bake bread for those orphans,' said his wife, 'that is what God has told me to tell you to do for him.' Of course, like a good husband, he did as his wife said and so next morning he arrived at exactly the right time to supply their breakfast! It was milk that was required on another occasion. So the milk cart just happened to break down outside and the contents were given to the children!

One-time prisoners, now saved, willingly go back to offer salvation to their former fellows. Men and women of ease and affluence give all they have to bring refugees relief. They bring medicine, agriculture, literacy and all of God's saving resources to bear on addiction, destitution and poverty. This does not simply mean that outward conditions change. God's beauty was certainly meant to be found in these, but more than that, human beings find by the presence of Jesus in their helpers a new release from inferiority, depression, anxiety, shame, resentment and fear. When human beings are saved from these ugly feelings, they can effectively begin a beautification campaign outside of themselves. On the other hand, social action without the saving presence of Jesus can increase the ugliness inside people. 'Without me you can do nothing,' said Jesus. He meant it and it is true.

God also has gifts to give to even the least advantaged so that all men can feel beautiful before him. In *Cinderella's Betrothal Gifts* Michael Griffiths gives the powerful suggestion that the gifts of the Holy Spirit found in 1 Corinthians 12 are given to the church as a kind of betrothal pledge, jewelry perhaps which is meant to be used for her adornment on the wedding day. Instead she sits like Cinderella amidst the ashes of institutions having forgotten that she is meant to be getting ready for the great day. Whether the jewels are words (word of knowledge, word of wisdom, prophecy, tongues, interpretation) or power (healings, faith, miracles, distinguishing of spirits) – to each one is given a valuable gift with which the whole body of Christ is beautified. The nondescript people of life – which covers most of us – now may become something beautiful and beautifying. You may be given the gift of singing beautifully in the Spirit, or the gift of faith for relief projects to the hungry, or the ministry of effective prayer for the sick, or the gift of speaking forth God's words fluently, even if apart from Christ you seemed to have few gifts.

This beauty which God wishes to place upon us is seen fully in Jesus and is recognised by even his most serious critics and opponents. Renan, a rationalistic scholar of the nineteenth century, called Luke's Gospel 'the most beautiful book in the world'. The story of Jesus is painted there with pure artistry.

Luke tells us more of the Lord's ministry, between his transfiguration in Caesarea Philippi and his entry into Jerusalem, than any other Gospel, (9:51–19:28). This is the period of what we might call the 'freedom march'. Jesus travelled throughout the whole length of Israel, ending at Jerusalem where he made his last challenge. This 'love' or 'liberation' march took about eight months, culminating in his crucifixion and resurrection in Jerusalem. Luke, a doctor, describes the beautiful effects in the lives of those who encountered Jesus as his freedom march progressed toward the most beautiful act in history – when the just and good one died for the unjust and unlovely. 'Love to the loveless shown that they might lovely be . . .'

Worksheet

Find an idea in each of these ten passages from this period, which is a 'beauty' Christ wishes to clothe us with:

1. Luke 10:25–37	6. Luke 15:11–32
2. Luke 10:38–42	7. Luke 16:19–31
3. Luke 11:5–13	8. Luke 17:11–19
4. Luke 11:27–28	9. Luke 18:9–14
5. Luke 12:31–34	10. Luke 19:1–10

'And Jesus said to him, "Salvation has come to this house today, for this man, also, is a descendent of Abraham. The Son of Man came to seek and to save the lost." ' (Luke 19:9–10, GNB)

7
Future salvation

So far we have thought about salvation in two ways – as an accomplished fact and as an ongoing process. In chapter two we saw that when we trusted in the Lord Jesus Christ, we were saved; an event now in our *past*. The letter of Titus puts it: 'But when the kindness and love of God our Saviour was revealed, he saved us. It was not because of any good deeds that we ourselves had done, but because of his own mercy that he saved us, through the Holy Spirit, who gives us new birth and new life by washing us' (Titus 3:4,5, GNB). Similarly, 2 Timothy 1:9,10 says, 'He saved us and called us to be his own people, not because of what we have done, but because of his own purpose and grace. He gave us this grace by means of Christ Jesus before the beginning of time, but now it has been revealed to us through the coming of our Saviour, Christ Jesus. He has ended the power of death and through the gospel has revealed immortal life' (GNB).

Also, we saw that the *present* saving process is still going on in us: 'For the message about Christ's death on the cross is nonsense to those who are being lost; but for us who *are being saved* it is God's power' (1 Corinthians 1:18, GNB). Compare this with 1 Timothy 1:15, 'This is a true saying, to be completely accepted and believed: Christ Jesus came into the world to save sinners' (GNB).

But there is also a *future* dimension to our salvation. This is the culmination of salvation's work when there will be a new heaven and earth at the return of our Lord Jesus Christ. He will firmly establish his already present kingdom and root out all that offends (Matthew 13:41). Just as in the Old Testament a saviour was also a judge (e.g. Judges 2:16; 4:4), so Jesus who came to save will only complete that salvation by judging the forces of sin and Satan which stand in opposition to him and rescuing his people. A saviour who judged in Old Testament days not only pronounced a verdict but also acted to make sure his judgement was effective, and so delivered the righteous and destroyed the oppressor.

This salvation in the future will be the wonderful summing up of all that God is doing in creation and human history. Those who are already being saved look forward to the day when their bodies will be completely saved by a resurrection which will give them bodies such as the one Jesus has now. So Paul says, 'We eagerly wait for our Saviour, the Lord Jesus Christ, to come from heaven. He will change our weak mortal bodies and make them like his own glorious body, using that power by which he is able to bring all things under his rule' (Philippians 3:20,21, GNB). He adds that this day of full salvation is now nearer than when we first believed (Romans 13:11).

It has been popular as a common criticism of Christianity to say that believers are waiting for this salvation as 'pie in the sky when they die'. Things are bad now but put up with everything that happens to you and one day you will be compensated in heaven. This easy dismissal of the Christian's hope has often come from political opponents, who claim that we should shake off our chains and claim a heaven on earth now by violent revolution, and cease being drugged by religion. The Christian, however, may reply that being saved now is a good slice of the pie for the present and is an assurance that there is a lot more to come in the future.

Our present experience of God's saving power flames our hope and anticipation of the future. It reminds us of God's rescue plan in history and assures us that it is – or that *he* is – on the way.

Christians have awakened to a new world in which the values of glory, honour and incorruption are paramount, (see Romans 2:7). That is, they begin to desire things to be beautiful, worth honouring, and with eternal value. They desire these in themselves and in others, and in God's world which is potentially full of them. It is clear from the story of

44

man's origin in Genesis 2 that he had a calling to take the raw material of nature and develop it to its full potential. Man and woman were put into a garden, a paradise, as a working model, so that they would see the orderliness and beauty that God wanted them to cultivate in the world outside as they obeyed God and 'filled up the earth and subdued it'. Since sin has disturbed God's intent for man and the universe, it is those bearing the gospel of salvation who leave impressions of beauty in their path. 'How beautiful on the mountains are the feet of those who bring good news, who proclaim peace, who bring good tidings, who proclaim salvation, who say to Zion, "Your God reigns!" ' (Isaiah 52:7, NIV). The bearers and proclaimers of God's salvation put their feet down on God's earth and reclaim that area for God's will to be done on it 'as it is in heaven'. This is how God's rule or kingdom is being re-established. Using the weapons of Christ's blood and truth against Satan and his evil (see chapter four on Deliverance) the church prays, proclaims and practises the eternal life of the coming kingdom of God and so changes this age. Salvation which is experienced in ourselves and preached through our mouths, then lived out in lives committed to doing God's will, will finally fill the earth. What God intended for his creation will be recovered. Man's original rebellion by which God lost his intended steward, vice-regent and developer of creation, and as a result the earth and its beautiful potential were marred, will on the day of Christ's reappearance be totally reversed, and men in Christ will reign over a regenerated and resurrected universe. The potential beauty of life in this recreated universe defies imagination. Some attempts to describe what is yet to be are made in the Bible, despite the limitations of our vocabulary and experience. Isaiah speaks of it in Isaiah 11:1–10 (GNB) as he sees Jesus, David's descendant, reigning in a future day:

> The royal line of David is like a tree that has been cut down; but just as new branches sprout from a stump, so a new king will arise from among David's descendants.
> The spirit of the Lord will give him wisdom,
>   and the knowledge and skill to rule his people.
> He will know the Lord's will and honour him,

and find pleasure in obeying him.
He will not judge by appearance or hearsay;
   he will judge the poor fairly
   and defend the rights of the helpless.
At his command the people will be punished,
   and evil persons will die.
He will rule his people with justice and integrity.
Wolves and sheep will live together in peace,
   and leopards will lie down with young goats.
Calves and lion cubs will feed together,
   and little children will take care of them.
Cows and bears will eat together,
   and their calves and cubs will lie down in peace.
Lions will eat straw as cattle do.
Even a baby will not be harmed
   if it plays near a poisonous snake;
On Zion, God's sacred hill,
   there will be nothing harmful or evil.
The land will be as full of knowledge of the Lord
   as the seas are full of water.

This beautiful picture of the coming kingdom of God is repeated all over the Old Testament especially in the prophetic books. Zechariah poetically paints the picture of a day when safety is on the streets of the new society, the generation gap has gone, there is freedom and leisure for games and happiness, all the races become one people and everything secular and mundane, even cooking pots, become sacred (Zechariah 8:3–8; 14:16–20). That sounds like good news, especially to those of us who live in places marred by ugliness or who spend much of our time at the kitchen sink! His prophecy reaches the pinnacle of all when he declares 'Then the Lord will be king over all the earth; everyone will worship him as God and know him by the same name' (Zechariah 14:9, GNB).

Just as the Old Testament speaks of the coming glory of God's eternal kingdom, so too the finale of the New Testament, and of the Bible itself, is found in the book of Revelation, chapters 21 and 22. There in the New Jerusalem, God's heavenly city, we see man living in fellowship with God in a glorious environment. Any attempt to describe what has not yet been is bound to be full of limitations, but there is enough in the following passage to meet our present aspirations and partial experience, to thrill us and to call us on to God's great end.

What God intended at creation when he made Eden with a garden, a river, gold and precious stones (Genesis 2:8–12) is now beautifully and finally expressed in the New Jerusalem where moral and spiritual realities are the matter of which the city is made.

> The Spirit . . . showed me Jerusalem, the Holy City, coming down out of heaven from God and shining with the glory of God . . . [The city itself was made of pure gold, as clear as glass. The foundation-stones of the city wall were adorned with all kinds of precious stones.]
>
> The angel showed me the river of the water of life sparkling like crystal, and coming from the throne of God and of the Lamb . . . Then the angel said to me, "These words are true and can be trusted. And the Lord God, who gives his Spirit to the prophets, has sent his angel to show his servants what must happen very soon."
>
> "Listen!" says Jesus, "I am coming soon! Happy are those who obey the prophetic words in this book!" (Revelation 21:10,11,18,19; 22:1,6,7, GNB)

Already in the previous chapter of Revelation (20:11–15) we see that the Judge's verdict has been given against all that clings to sin, Satan and death. The rubbish heap belonging to the heavenly city is outside the gates and anyone not written in the book of life – the city's register – is cast into the lake of fire. This is the final judgement. Tragically, God has to pass verdict on our lives. Those clinging on to sin and death receive what they demand. They refuse to be written up for life. Ultimately, God says sadly – if you will not do my will, then yours will have to be done. In the last analysis, if we will not have God, the Father of our Lord Jesus Christ, *now*, why should we want him *then*? The one judging from the great white throne (Revelation 20:11) is none other than Christ, the crucified, who is the man crowned with honour and glory and who was not allowed to see corruption (Hebrews 2:9; Acts 2:27). If we do not seek or want what is honourable, glorious or eternal now (see Romans 2:7), why should we want it or him on that day? Heaven would be obnoxious to a person choosing lust, hate, self-interest and pride. All – the saved and the lost – will agree with God's verdict when Jesus returns. The saved who enter into the salvation city will declare that it was all because of God's free gift and mercy that they are there. Peter writes in his first epistle:

> 'Let us give thanks to the God and Father of our Lord Jesus Christ! Because of his great mercy he gave us new life by raising Jesus Christ from death. This fills us with a living hope, and so we look forward to possessing the rich blessings that God keeps for his people. He keeps them for you in heaven, where they cannot decay or spoil or fade away. They are for you, who through faith are kept safe by God's power for the salvation which is ready to be revealed at the end of time' (1 Peter 1:3–5, GNB).

Training for reigning

Peter speaks of the trial of our faith. While we are being saved waiting for our final salvation, we are in training and so naturally there are tests. Our training is to enable us to reign with Christ in the recovered universe which will be functioning as God originally intended it to.

Creation has lost its purpose and is in the slavery of decay (Romans 8:18–21). This was due to man's revolt. Dominion and authority had been delegated to man and woman together at their creation (Genesis 1:28) as they were told to fill the earth and subdue it. When sin entered the world, through the first man, Adam, creation revolted against humans. Dominion is restored over the earth only through the new humanity or 'second man' as Jesus is called. Like Adam, Jesus also has his offspring but they are spiritual children, people who are born again. We Christians are a new humanity to fill the earth with his authority, that is, with his name (John 14:12–14).

We train for God's kingdom by learning to live, work and speak in the power of his name, bringing his power and influence to bear in every situation.

We are to reign in life by one, Jesus Christ (Romans 5:17), that is we live victoriously rather than struggling with defeat. In so reigning in life by him now we are learning to reign in the future with him. A precise translation of Romans 8:17 would be, 'And if children, then heirs, heirs indeed of God but joint heirs with Christ, if so be that we endure with him that we may be also glorified together.' Similarly 2 Timothy 2:12 says, 'If we endure, we shall reign with him.'

When we began thinking about salvation in chapter one of this book we had this diagram:

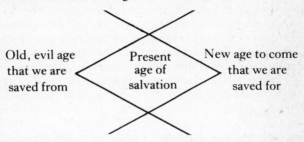

Old, evil age that we are saved from

Present age of salvation

New age to come that we are saved for

showing how this great future age for which we hope has now invaded our present scene. Our present training programme is not only preparing us for the future reign with Christ but it is also giving us the opportunity to bring that 'salvation age' fully into the world. We do this in at least three ways. We:

Preach it in: 'This Good News about the Kingdom will be preached through all the world for a witness to all mankind; and then the end will come' (Matthew 24:14, GNB, see also Matthew 28:18–20).

Pray it in: 'May your Kingdom come' (Matthew 6:10) is the first prayer of the New Testament and 'Come Lord Jesus' (Revelation 22:20) is the last prayer of the New Testament.

Practise it in: 'What kind of people should you be? Your lives should be holy and dedicated to God, as you wait for the Day of God and do your best to make it come soon' (2 Peter 3:11,12, GNB).

Just as a loving bridegroom will only come to take his bride to the wedding day when she wants to go and would not drag her to the wedding against her will, so Christ comes for his bride the church when she is longing and living for his return (Revelation 19:7).

As we live 'salvation-style' lives anticipating the coming age we not only hasten the coming of that age, we effect a salvaging programme that brings God's salvation power to others. This salvation operation flows from Christ through the church to people's spirits, setting them free from the oppression of Satan; to human souls as the love of Christ brings wholeness to fractured emotions and unhealthy minds; and to bodies as saving health is received. Then it flows into relationships and the way we relate to each other in all areas of life, the church, the domestic scene, work and society. These realms are invaded by the saving power of Christ through men and women of faith, releasing saving health to all the nations. It may be too much to expect the fullness of heaven to be expressed on an unregenerate earth, even though the beauty of our life together in the body of Christ might approximate to this sometimes! But we do expect to transform everything we touch with God's salvation, including the structure of people's lives, affirming them as persons, even if they do not become Christians.

In the Old Testament days, Israel was meant to show this true kind of society. Yet despite the sophisticated humanitarian legislation which God gave them to live by (some of it far in advance of even the most enlightened legislation of the twentieth century) the Israelites of Isaiah's day disobeyed and exploited one another.

Because of their failure to 'salt' society with their godliness and justice, Isaiah is told to show the people their sin and chapters 58–61 show us God's desire for the salvation of society. In order to reveal the people's callousness and inhumanity he has to strip off the hypocritical garments of religion from the people (Isaiah 58:1–5) – for they were extremely good at religious meetings, faces, postures, clothes, debates and strifes yet at the same time were experts in social *un*righteousness. This disease of religiosity also afflicts the present day people of God. We demonstrate that we don't want heaven and its true society by producing and perpetuating an unjust hell on earth now, exploiting and misusing one another. In Isaiah 58:6,7 (NIV) Isaiah describes 'true religion':

Is not this the kind of fasting I have chosen:
    to loose the chains of injustice
        and untie the cords of the yoke,

to set the oppressed free
    and break every yoke?
Is it not to share your food with the hungry
    and to provide the poor wanderer with shelter –
when you see the naked, to clothe him,
    and not to turn away from your own flesh and blood?

Jesus must have had these verses in mind when he fed the thousands and gave to the poor, when he taught 'if you have a party invite those who are too disadvantaged to repay you'. As he told the story of the rich man and Lazarus, he was making the point that we cannot hide away from our fellow men and women, and in the last judgement he tells us that he will ask if we have clothed him by clothing the naked (Mark 8:19,20; John 13:29; Luke 14:12–14; 16:19–31; Matthew 25:43).

There are further allusions made by Jesus to this chapter 58 of Isaiah. When Jesus in Matthew 5:13–16 calls the church, salt, light and a city set on a hill he is alluding to Isaiah 58:8–12. Isaiah's message is that light and health (i.e. salt for healing) will break forth and the city be rebuilt when Israel is prepared to take social salvation seriously.

It is not, cries the prophet (Isaiah 59:1,2), that God cannot save or that his arm is short; it is the people's sin that keeps God from hearing them. Then follows (Isaiah 59:3–11) a list of sin, crime and injustice, with vivid metaphors of satanic activity amongst the community in terms of vipers and spiders' webs, culminating with the cry in verse 11: 'We look for justice, and there is none; for salvation, but it is far from us' (RSV). Consequently, God acts (Isaiah 59:12–17), for there is no one to intercede for the people in their state of unrighteousness. He comes to save them wearing armour for the battle against evil. This intervention by God, and the armour he wears, is shown to us again in Ephesians 6:10–18 where the intervention is Christ's invasion and the armour is worn by his body the church. The church also battles against all forms of oppression bringing God's salvation in the power of his Spirit, beginning with Satan himself and never resting content in the presence of any form of exploitation and bondage. The coming of the Holy Spirit is seen (Isaiah 59:19,21) as is world evangelisation, and the new covenant of the Spirit. Chapter 60 glows with the light of a new day and a new Jerusalem, seen in all its salvation splendour. Finally, the words used by Jesus himself to proclaim his kingdom's manifesto bring the whole prophetic passage to a climax in a declaration of liberty (Isaiah 61:1,2, NIV):

> The Spirit of the Sovereign LORD is on me,
> because the LORD has anointed me
> to preach good news to the poor.
> He has sent me to bind up the broken-hearted,
>   to proclaim freedom for the captives
>   and release for the prisoners,
> to proclaim the year of the Lord's favour
>   and the day of vengeance of our God,
> to comfort all who mourn . . .

This vision of God's new and true society and of the way in which by the Holy Spirit it has invaded our present age has brought to birth in God's people a desire to express what is fundamental in God's heart for mankind. This is why true Christians down through the ages have expressed their commitment to God's kingdom by bringing the benefits of that kingdom into the world around them. Hospitals, schools and orphanages were born out of God's salvation for man. Modern democracy was the product of the Christian non-conformist conscience, and godly scientists like Kepler, Newton and Boyle gave scientific technology to the world; while the famous Cavendish Scientific Laboratory has a quotation from the Bible, 'The works of the Lord are great, sought out of all them that have pleasure therein' (Psalm 111:2) over its doors. The great evangelist John Wesley, in addition to his preaching, ran an employment exchange, wrote text books to reach the poor, founded many welfare institutions and wrote his last letter to Wilberforce encouraging him in his fight against slavery. William Wilberforce spent forty years of his parliamentary life bringing in legislation to remove slavery. This was because his experience of salvation expressed itself in this and other areas. Of the successes of the group of evangelical Christians to which Wilberforce belonged and which effected many social and political changes the celebrated historian G. M. Trevelyan wrote, 'Mankind had been successfully lifted on to a higher plane by the energy of good men and the world breathed a kindlier air.'

Many areas of modern life are what they are in the benefits they bring mankind because salvation working through Christians has conceived and brought forth change or invaded areas of government, unions, law courts, art and social work procedures. Christians today are in the battle against famine, leading in refugee and relief work and have spearheaded many breakthroughs against poverty and disease. W. E. H. Lecky was not a believer but was an outstanding historian. He writes:

> The character of Jesus has not only been the highest pattern of virtue, but the strongest incentive to its practice, and has exerted so deep an influence that it may be truly said, that the simple record of three short years of active life has done more to regenerate and to soften mankind, than all the disquisitions of philosophers and than all the exhortations of moralists.

Such is the effect of God's salvation entering into individual men and women and from them moving out into the world of social and political action, arts, science and philosophy. Christians do not anticipate creating a heaven on earth, but they do know and believe that God's salvation, which is to come, is so powerful that it has overflowed and broken into this age now. We are, as Hebrews 6:5 puts it, tasting the powers of the age to come. We expect to honour and respect God's creation by relieving and caring for the groaning universe till its final salvation comes from heaven at the coming of our Lord Jesus Christ.

Paul, in Titus 2:11–14, sums up the present programme of God's salvation and its relationship to his future intervention through our Saviour Jesus Christ to save the earth, in these words (GNB):

> For God has revealed his grace for the salvation of all mankind. That grace instructs us to give up ungodly living and worldly passions, and to live self-controlled, upright and godly lives in this world, as we wait for the blessed Day we hope for, when the glory of our great God and Saviour Jesus Christ will appear. He gave himself for us, to rescue us from all wickedness and to make us a pure people who belong to him alone and are eager to do good.

Worksheet

1. Matthew's Gospel could be called the Gospel of the Kingdom, the word 'kingdom' appearing more times than any other. In chapter 13 find the seven parables of the kingdom and analyse the two phases of the secret kingdom and the open kingdom, corresponding to our present salvation and our future salvation.

2. Each of the chapters of 1 and 2 Thessalonians (with the exception of 2 Thessalonians 3) contains a reference to the second coming of Jesus. Find the references and list the things they tell us about the second coming.

8

Saved by baptism?

Most people are aware that baptism is the mark or badge of a Christian. In many countries, secret believers are tolerated until they are baptised and from then on they suffer persecution. Other societies are more tolerant and just ignore the practice, even if they have themselves been baptised in infancy.

However, in both situations, there are large numbers of people who have the mistaken idea that it is baptism which makes the Christian, or saves the person. Two verses in the Bible might seem to support this idea. 1 Peter 3:21 uses the phrase: 'Baptism, which now saves you' and Mark 16:16: 'Whoever believes and is baptised shall be saved'.

We must look at both these verses and ask what they are really saying. How important is baptism to salvation, and why are they connected at all? Where does faith come in when Paul says 'by grace are you saved, through faith'?

The New Testament speaks of baptism as pictures of three Old Testament events, which are symbols of the meaning that Jesus has brought into the action of baptism.

1 Crossing the Red Sea

In 1 Corinthians 10:1–13 Paul shows that the Exodus event when the Red Sea was miraculously passed through by the Israelites is an example for us Christians. There they were all baptised as followers of Moses in the cloud and in the sea, as they went through the water. Paul's application of this story demonstrates that, even if we have begun the Christian life and been baptised into Christ, we must still be aware of the temptations which are common to man and use the way of escape God gives to overcome.

We have already seen that passing through the Red Sea was called a salvation and the Israelites were saved by the drowning of their enemies (Exodus 14:13). Moses celebrated this deliverance baptism in song (Exodus 15:1–3). But Paul has warned us that with many of the Israelites God was not well pleased. The watery event of baptism did not create in itself the faith to resist temptation. Again in the New Testament, Jude introduces his epistle by saying he is going to speak of salvation then refers to this same event of the Exodus but adds that, having saved the people out of the land of Egypt, God destroyed those who did not believe. To be saved and continue being saved required faith, otherwise the Red Sea 'baptism' was worthless. Ongoing faith was all-important, and baptism was merely the symbol of their deliverance, that they were cut off from their enemies.

2   Noah and the Flood

Peter, in his first epistle (3:20–23, GNB) certainly says we are saved by baptism but continues by qualifying his statement 'saved by water' in this way: 'It is not the washing away of bodily dirt, but the promise made to God from a good conscience. It saves you through the resurrection of Jesus Christ.' There can be little doubt that it is not the literal water or symbol itself, but the spiritual reality of a promise or faith-commitment embracing Christ's resurrection that brings salvation to us.

Noah's work saved his family from the consequences of God's judgement on sin. As the ark came safely through to a new-washed world, so now we come through into a fresh life – a life in which we share in the resurrection life of Jesus by faith in Christ's work on the cross. We are Jesus Christ's family and so, like Noah's, are saved. Christ's work, like Noah's, is unsinkable for those who trust him and enter in. Many people have said to me when they have received Christ by faith: 'I feel so washed' or 'I've never felt so clean in all my life'. Baptism, like the *flood*, symbolises the *washing away* of sins to freshen us up for a new clean life.

3   Adam and his death

Paul speaks a lot about Adam in Romans 5, and how he let sin into the world so that death followed on behind. God had said, 'In the day you eat of it (the forbidden fruit) you will surely die.' Having disobeyed Adam died; so too have all others, since all have sinned (Romans 5:12). Equally, he spells out how Christ's act of righteousness on the cross has made us right with God and has brought life to all men. As he proceeds into chapter 6 he explains that baptism means that we have passed from the realm of Adam and death by being buried and resurrected in Christ. The only thing to do with a dead person is to bury him. However good or pleasant we are, we have to acknowledge that we are only fit for death, and so we are 'buried' by baptism into Christ's death. However, just as Christ rose from the dead, so we too in him are 'raised' from the baptismal water into a new kind of life (Romans 6:3,4). Baptism is a powerful, positive way of saying to God, man and the devil that you are unable to save yourself and are fit to die, and therefore you offer yourself to be buried. In Jesus' name you are buried, meaning that you trust his death to bring you out into life.

When Adam sinned, God first promised a Saviour: 'And I will put enmity between you and the woman, and between your offspring and hers; he will crush your head and you will strike his heel' (Genesis 3:15, NIV). Then God pronounced Adam's death sentence. Adam responded in faith, calling his wife 'Eve', that is, 'living', showing that he trusted the promise of life given by God. It was a *burial*, not in despair and hopelessness, but where there was faith in the promised Christ. So water baptism today is effective not by a literal death but by living faith in Jesus.

Salvation, then, as symbolised in the act of water baptism, is:

(a) A sea to cut off my enemies, that is, sin and Satan.
'You will hurl all our iniquities into the depths of the sea.'   (Micah 7:19, NIV)

(b) A flood to wash me from my sin and make me clean and acceptable to God.

'Get up and be baptised and have your sins washed away by praying to him.' (Acts 22:16, GNB)

(c) A burial to save me from my self that is fit only to die.

'When you were baptised you were buried with Christ, and in baptism you were also raised with Christ through your faith . . .' (Colossians 2:12, GNB)

What then can Mark 16:15 mean: 'He who believes *and* is baptised shall be saved'? I remember a great missionary of the first half of the twentieth century, Willie Burton, speaking on this passage at a meeting. He had seen hundreds of churches come into being in Africa, with many healings and signs and wonders in his ministry. He quietly read the passage, unobtrusively adding his own words as though they were there in the text, though of course we all realised they were not. The italicised words are his addition.

Jesus said to them 'Go throughout the whole world and preach the gospel to all mankind. Whoever believes and is baptised will be saved; whoever does not believe will be condemned, *whether he is baptised or not*!'

Of course we all smiled, realising what he had done, but also noting the point he clearly made, that baptism apart from faith is worthless. It is faith that brings a man into the power of the good news of Jesus Christ and the experience of being saved. The simple way of expressing this faith to the world, the flesh and the devil, and not least to God and his church, is to be baptised. It is the way the people of God (one of whom would baptise you outwardly) recognise that you are a true believer.

Perhaps you have never been baptised at any time in your life. Now that you are a believer you should openly acknowledge this and stand with God's people, letting them also stand with you, in this act of obedience. As you do so, you will be declaring that 'It is by God's grace that you have been saved through faith. It is not the result of your own efforts, but God's gift, so that no one can boast about it' (Ephesians 2:8,9, GNB).

Worksheet

Read:

Matthew 3:13–16; 28:19.
John 4:1,2.
Acts 2:38–41; 8:12–16; 8:36; 9:18; 10:47,48; 16:15,33;
    18:8; 19:3–5; 22:16.
Romans 6:3,4.
1 Corinthians 1:14–17.
Galatians 3:27.

9
How may I be saved?

We are not saved in any tense – past, present or future – or in any sphere – spirit, soul, body, church or world – by baptism. This we saw in the last chapter. Neither are we saved by our own works as the last verses quoted in that chapter also assert.

Clearly we are saved by Jesus for he is the Saviour of the world as the people of Samaria acknowledged when they trusted Christ, saying to the woman, 'We believe now, not because of what you said, but because we ourselves have heard him, and we know that he really is the Saviour of the world' (John 4:42, GNB).

But you may be asking, 'What is my part then? What do I have to do? What makes the difference between those who are dying and those who are being saved?' John 3:16,17 (GNB) says: 'For God loved the world so much that he gave his only Son, so that everyone who believes in him may not die but have eternal life. For God did not send his Son into the world to be its judge, but to be its saviour.'

If the gift of salvation is for the whole world, why are some saved and some not? If it is a gift, what makes the difference between the haves and have nots? Of course the answer clearly is faith. Faith or trust in Christ, makes the distinction.

It is faith which receives the gift of God; accepts and trusts God's offer of Jesus.

Now there is a kind of faith which is merely a credal statement of orthodox Christian doctrine, not an actual reception of Christ into one's life, nor a commitment to a relationship with somebody who is really there. But Jesus is genuinely alive and very much with us. Just as the disciple

Thomas later realised that on the very occasion he was saying, 'Unless I see the scars of the nails in his hands and put my finger on those scars and my hand in his side, I will not believe', Jesus must have been there listening, for he quotes it all back to him eight days later. On the second occasion, Jesus said, 'Put your finger here, and look at my hands; then stretch out your hand and put it in my side. Stop your doubting, and believe!'

Thomas saw him and believed, and yet even this kind of faith is not the best. 'How happy are those who believe without seeing me!' added Jesus.

It is a much happier and more blessed thing to believe when you do not see the evidence before your eyes. This kind of faith brings more answers to prayer and a greater intimacy with our Lord. Thomas did not have an advantage over us because he could see Jesus in the flesh. We are more advantaged because trusting when we can't see brings much happiness and God blesses such faith with results.

However, even faith in the actual existence of Jesus – that he is really there – is not enough to save us. James says the demons believe like this in God but it makes no difference as to their state of life or eternal destiny. This faith is a dead faith since it does nothing (see James 2:17,20,26). Some people are confused at this, for they think that faith means doing nothing because Paul says we are saved by faith, not works. The simple distinction to notice is this: Paul means the works *of the law*. He says we are saved by faith apart from the deeds of the law (Romans 3:28). The works of the law are not the same as the works of faith. The works of the law are the Ten Commandments, religious activities and rituals as taught in the Law of Moses. No one has ever kept all of them and earned salvation. On the other hand, James gives two examples of persons who had works of faith – Abraham when he offered up Isaac, and Rahab the harlot. Neither case seems much of a candidate for keeping the law (James 2:21–25) since one would have committed murder and the other was a liar. But both had works of faith. Abraham obeyed, trusting that God would raise Isaac from the dead, and Rahab lied and hid the spies who came to her in Jericho as an expression of her real faith. If she had said, 'I really do believe God is going to give the Israelites the land, but the police are at the door. I must now hand you over to them,' she certainly would have lacked real faith, in the biblical sense, quite apart from the fact that her story would not have gone down in scripture and her life would have been lost in the fall of Jericho. She might have claimed a kind of 'believism' or even a credal statement but not a real trust. The fact that she had a real trust in the God of Israel was seen in her willingness to stake everything on his intervention and support even if her life was threatened because she would appear a traitor. Real faith that saves is that which shows by its actions that it is faith. So Rahab acted out her faith in hiding the spies.

Perhaps one of the clearest places in the New Testament for learning real faith is Romans 10. In verse 17 (GNB) Paul says: 'Faith comes from hearing the message, and the message comes through preaching Christ.' Where do we first hear the word of Christ? Well, of course it is the Bible message (Paul quotes the Old Testament in vs. 18–21) which is fulfilled in Jesus and which points always to our Lord Jesus Christ. So even the word of God through Moses in Deuteronomy 30:11–14 is a word of Christ. Paul quotes these verses in Romans 10:8. He says, in effect: 'Don't say Christ the word is in heaven – a long way away – or in the abyss – inaccessible. He is near each one, even in your heart and in your mouth.' So 'it is by our faith that we are put right with God; it is by our confession that we are saved. The scripture says, "Whoever believes in him will not be disappointed"' (Romans 10:10,11, GNB).

Real, living, saving faith is not far away from any one of us. It is possible, for the word is near our mouths and near our hearts. Faith comes by hearing the word of Christ and opening our hearts – even only a little – and our mouths, just a fraction will do. This word which is Jesus will then invade our heart enabling us to believe, and fill our mouths inspiring us to confess our salvation.

Many times I have seen people begin to pray in uncertainty while saying they are not ready yet to be saved, but before they have prayed more than a few sentences they are praying with more confidence and expectancy, and before long they are asking the Lord that they might be saved. This is because Christ is at work, putting his word into their mouth and his message into their hearts.

If we believe by opening our hearts in trust to the living Christ then of course we believe that God has raised him from the dead. We are saying, 'You are there to come into my life.' We are believing in the God who is bigger than death and has beaten it in his son, Jesus Christ. Christ is here, helping me to believe. If I confess with my mouth Jesus as Lord, his word in my mouth is calling on him to take my life and remake it so that I live in his world his way. Saving faith is faith in a God of the miraculous who has defeated death, and a trust in his lordship which I intend to obey.

His salvation is now mine but it is also for the whole world. 'Everyone who calls out to the Lord for help will be saved' (Romans 10:13, GNB). This is because God loved the world (John 3:16) and is the Saviour of all especially those who believe (1 Timothy 4:10). Christ is the Lamb of God who takes away the sin of the world (John 1:29) and who gave himself a ransom for all (1 Tim. 2:6), and his good news must be preached in all the world before the end shall come (Matthew 24:14).

Some years ago two missionaries sold themselves into slavery in the West Indian plantations in order to reach the slaves with salvation. As their ship left the shores of Europe, one was heard to cry out the words which became the slogan of their Moravian Church Mission: 'That the Lamb that was slain might receive the reward of his sufferings!' Every man in the world owes it to Jesus to call him Lord and to believe in his heart God has raised him from the dead. Christ has paid for that with his life, and deserves the reward of his sufferings. God has raised him from the dead so that all people can believe. He is near their hearts and mouths that they might believe. Out of love for him, let us not be afraid to tell men and women everywhere that they may be saved.